Inside the Head of a Conch Woman

Inside the Head of a Conch Woman

J. M. Varela

Inside the Head of a Conch Woman
© 2011 by J. M. Varela
All rights reserved
Reproduction of this book or any part thereof is prohibited, except
    for quotation for review purposes, without express permission
    of the author and publisher.

Cover painting by Linda Cabrera
Drawing accompanying "Old King Philip" by Melinda Blair

Printed in the United States of America

ISBN 978-1-936818-25-9
LCCN 2011943492

SeaStory Press
305 Whitehead St. #1
Key West, Florida 33040
www.seastorypress.com

ACKNOWLEDGMENTS

To my husband, Douglas Gregory, who financed this publication and first muttered the book title after listening to several Conch women all talking at the same time about different subjects on an early morning walk to Dennis Pharmacy. The Conch chatter left him worn out and amazed when he commented, "I feel like I've been inside the head of a Conch woman."

Cover art is by Linda Cabrera who preserves lost scenes from our Key West past in oil and canvas.

Poems

A Tribute To All Poets...ix

People 1

Island Girl 2
Old King Philip..4
Carolina Shrimpers...6
Katie's Tune 8
A Poem For Miss Beulah 9
Winter Visitors 12
The Touristos Are Coming 14
The Jedi Attorney..16
Nicaraguan Serenade..18
Kli Kli 20
Clouds 22
Sweet Lorraine...24
I Can See Cuba From My House 26
Father Anthony 27
Child at Play..28

Places and Events......................................29

It's Cool Inside 30
Key West Sunset..32
House of Dreams...33
October Smoke 34
Two Windows and a Door 36
Battle Hymn of the Harbor Reef 38
Diamonds on the Water 40
Bolita Vacations...42
Louisiana 2005..44
Turtle Mystery Of 1948...46

Philosophy 49

Reality & Dreams..50

vi

Poems

Dance On 51
Ride the Wind 52
Midnight Butterfly 54
Morning Star 55
The Storm 56
Safe Harbor 57
Listen To The Night 58
If I Were A Tree 60
Mother Earth Said, AHH 61

Romance 63

Romancing the Tides 64
Ice Cream on a Hot Sidewalk 66
Poof 68
We Are One 70
Until We Meet Again 71
Capture 72
Phoenix 73
Intruder 74
Getting Over Him 75
When Love Dies In The Tropics 76
Drifting 78
M E N 79

Holidays 81

December Lights 82
Christmas Magic 84

The End 85

Bridges 86
About the Author 87

A Tribute To All Poets

They attempt the impossible,
Putting thoughts into words.
It's almost like trying to fly
When you're not even a bird.
For how does one define
The vast universe
In the mere written word?
Yet, each age has it poets.
They still clamor to be heard.
So pen of mine take wings tonight,
And write upon the sky.
That poets leave their souls in ink.
They never really die.

1976
Guild Hall

People

Island Girl

I'm an island girl, born and bred.
Drunk on too much sunshine,
Like most Conchs
I'm a little light in the head.

I put Key Lime juice on fried chicken
And on avocado salad too.
Hate wearing panty hose,
Hate wearing shoes.

I'm happiest when walking
Barefoot in the sand,
With the sun and salty
Breezes caressing my face.
Don't think I'd enjoy living
Quite as much in any other place.

I've lived through hurricanes, corrupt politicians
And days of unending rains.
The foot of Solares Hill
Was my youthful stomping ground.
Where New Orleans style funerals
And Cuban Conga lines
Gave me an ear for African rhythms
And other soulful sounds.

At the elbows of Conch Grandmas
I learned the art of making chowders
And Guava Duff.
Once you've tasted our island dishes,
You'll never be able to get enough.

Uncles who made a living harvesting the sea,
Taught me to respect with awe
The ocean's many melodies.
The constant ebb and flow
Of our multi-colored waters
Taught me the meaning of
Life's cycles, peace and harmony.

So Big City Girls in your
High heels and stockings
Your way of life,
I'm really not knocking.
You can have your fancy stores,
Smog alerts and traffic jams.
I'm happy to be a simple Island Girl
Top that, if you can . . .

1973

Old King Philip

Old King Philip is a sorry old soul.
A drunken old soul is he.
He sits on a bench,
Drinking all day.
Doesn't even have to get up to pee.

Under the spreading Banyan tree
By a church on a Key West Street
His life of empty wine bottles
Lay around his dirty feet.

Some People laugh and call him names
As they pass him by.
Cursing his wretched way of life.
Hoping that he'll hurry up and die.

On the first of the month
Welfare checks arrive
Marked "General Delivery."
He gets one good drunk from his
And wakes up in the local pokey.

A few days rest, good food and a bath,
Back out into the world he goes,
Swearing that this time
He'll never drink again.
But, park benches are lonely
And Banyan trees don't keep you dry
When it rains.
So Old King Philip
Falls off the wagon again.

Someday, they'll find this King of Winos
Dead under a bush somewhere.
Or on the steps of Carpenters' Hall.
They'll bury him on pauper's hill
In a hastily dug grave so small.
No one will weep his parting.
Except perhaps the Banyan tree
Now so quiet and still.

Published in Key West Ghosts, An Anthology of Key West Poetry, *1976*

Carolina Shrimpers

They migrate here each year
From southern swamps and fishing towns
    Carolina Shrimpers.
In the warm, clear Caribbean waters
That surround this tiny island,
They cast their hungry nets down.

Some will bring their sons along.
They know that the ocean
Offers an education
Not found in ordinary classrooms.
After weeks of rolling decks
And lonely star lit nights,
He will become attuned
To Neptune's song.

Young hands, callused and stained
By the arduous task of harvesting the sea
Proudly proclaim that he now belongs
To a special breed of men.

When they have had their fill
Of Pink Gold and waterfront bars,
They return to home fires
On sultry Carolina shores.

Every now and then one will remain.
Maybe he has been captured
By Key West's sleepy, manana charm.
Perhaps he's drunk from
Too much sunshine.
Or, better yet, hypnotized
By some island girl's inviting arms.

But a lady's arms cannot hold a
    Carolina Shrimper
For salt water flows through his veins.
Enticed by the sound of the waves
And the scent of salty air,
When the tide moves out
He will go with it – to his real love,
        His real home
    To the Sea
        To the Sea

Written in honor of Capt. Douglas R. Gregory, Sr
January 17, 1926 – March 22, 2004
and Douglas R. Gregory, Jr.
1977

Katie's Tune

She was a lady of the night.
Seeking love in all the wrong places.
The many men she's known
Throughout the years
Are now blurred into unnamed faces.
Her charms are dried and withered with age.
Her soul no longer shines.
The bar people know her only as "Katie."
And for her grave she pines.
She still haunts the local taverns.
A graying creature of the night.
Going through that ageless routine
Of looking for a trick to turn.
When asleep her dreams take her back
To gayer times she knew.
When young men were drawn to her doorstep,
Eager to pay for her body's use.
Look for her on Duval Street
Or, at Big Daddy's in the afternoon.
When you hear the strains
Of a sad and forgotten song,
You'll know its Katie's Tune.

1975

A Poem For Miss Beulah
(Reflections of Key West History & Conch Grandmothers)

In the long ago hot summers
You could find her
Pigtails bouncing
As she skipped rope barefoot
On dirt sidewalks
That once lined Division Street
Life was so simple then.

As she grew through her childhood
On this small Caribbean island,
The town grew with her.

These were the days
Of nick names and Sunday promenades
On Duval Street
Where every face you passed
Was a friendly one.
Somehow she survived
High top shoes, chaperons
And strict curfews.

As she grew into a
Lovely young woman,
The town grew with her.

Then came the time
Of wedding bells, Octagon soap
And babies so eager to be born.
Her life was filled with
Laundry and island cooking
Too busy to be forlorn.

Her husband lost his job
Like so many others
During the Great Depression.
So she took in ironing
And sold benny cakes door to door.
But, Conch men don't stay idle for too long
With the help of President Roosevelt's WPA
They soon had jobs again.

The day came when
The sleepy fishing village
Woke up to help the nation
Prepare for World War II.
These were the days when the island's economy
Kept pace with the 8 and 4 o'clock
Whistle of the navy yard.

With money in their pockets
A new house they did buy
Built on the out skirts of old town
Where a salt pond once lie.
CBS they called it,
A concrete block structure
With window screens and air conditioning.

Sometimes late at night
When she could not sleep,
She fondly remembered the
Gingerbread wood trim
And cool high ceilings
Of the old Conch homestead
She sold to 'strangas.'
These were the times
She asked herself
'Had life really improved?'

As she grew
Into a mature woman
The town grew with her.

Now the present is at hand.
How times have changed.
So many new faces
Known only by last names.
Her hair has turned gray
How the years slipped away.

As she grew
Into a graceful elder woman,
The town aged with her.

Conch grandmothers
Like the island they call The Rock,
Possess strength borne from hard times,
The quiet wisdom of their age,
And the love of everyone
Who knows them.

*Presented to Mrs. Beulah Demerrit upon her retirement from
Monroe County government
6/28/78*

Winter Visitors

You can not claim her as your own.
You do not live here all year long.
You only visit for awhile
And leave us when the weather
Does not smile.

You only enjoy the good times
Wearing LL Bean shoes and sweater vests.
You don't know what it means
To try to shower upstairs
In barely trickling warm water
To feel the humidity sit on your chest.

You can not claim her as your own
Until you make this place your home.
You only vacation with your friends
And leave us when the cool breezes end.

Like a right of passage
Some would say,
You must suffer, you must stay
During times of summer heat
Mosquito plagues and bugs that creep.

Not til you've weathered a storms
Shuttered windows – no A/C,
Can you say you're one of us.
By surviving the bad times
You earn our trust.

Leave your carpet bags up there
We have no need for them here.
Say hello to island life
Full of summer doldrums, heat and strife

Oh, you bring us so much culture
Theater, symphonies,
Funding raising parties and social teas
Playing crochet on the lawn
Its much too much, makes me yawn.

When the temperature reaches 92
And your feet sweat in those LL Bean shoes,
Delta whisks you away from the melting pot
To regions green and not so hot.

We whisper a heart-felt good-bye
Clean up the messes you left behind.
With a sigh of relief we settle in
To make this island home
Ours   alone   again.

You cannot claim her your own
You do not live here all year long.

4/4/2007

The Touristos Are Coming

When Indian summer sunsets
Linger longer than they should.
And pumpkin colored skies
Announce the advent of autumn.
If you've got sands in your shoes,
You will feel IT.
IT begins with a dull, creeping sensation
That's hard to put your finger on at first,
Similar to the chilly under currents
That run beneath the Gulf Stream.
IT becomes more evident day by day.
As we see the subtle Caribbean hints
Of changing seasons.
Now, IT takes on the semblance
Of a constant annoyance
Like a pesky mosquito that just
Won't go away.
The island pace picks up.
The sleepy fishing village awakens,
Takes a deep breath,
And with a busy bustling so often
Associated with storm warnings,
Battens down for a different
Kind of hurricane.
At night you can almost hear IT
Like a swarm of locust
Way off in the distance, humming.
THE TOURISTOS ARE COMING.
THE TOURISTOS ARE COMING.
The chorus reaches its climax
Round about the same time

That the first snow falls in the
Lake Erie region.
Then IT happens
Yes, IT definitely is upon us
For another year
TOURIST SEASON IS HERE.

Call on your reserves of patience
For you will need it.
A drive into town becomes
A three ring circus.
The stores, restaurants and beaches
Are no longer ours.
White skins, baked and oiled
Proclaim that foreigners
Have invaded our home land.
But, the sounds of clanging
Cash registers do help
To ease the pain.

So we politely endure the seize.
Fortified by the knowledge
That the spring will bring
A peaceful return to our island hide-a-way.

When this temporary insanity is finally spent.
A sign of relief is heard throughout the island.
And Key West is ours, alone again.

1977 Before the Monroe County Tourist Development Council

The Jedi Attorney

Something is a blowin' on Simonton Street
But it's not powdery white or smokey Grey.
It's brown, dense and awful smelly.
The more you stir it – The more it stinks.

The Federales couldn't catch the slimy con man
Or his dickhead client
So they spun a tall tale
Of power and corruption
And went after the consolation prize instead:
The Jedi Attorney.

Their net of immunity covered far and wide
Shielding the con man, the dickhead and even the slut.
Jurors slumped in their chairs
After weeks of monotonous testimony
Broken only by one frog-like "ribbit"
Muttered by The Jedi Attorney.

When the dirty deed was done,
The Jedi Attorney was crucified,
Shackled and photographed for the morning news.
I walked from the Federal Courthouse
Stunned, In disbelief.
Down Caroline to Duval Street.
Spring break scooters honked,
Music flowed from the bars
The sun felt warm and forgiving.

The Federal prosecutor loaded her car
With boxes of legal briefs and evidence
For the long journey home through the Keys.
Thump,   thump,   thump

Rubber tires hummed a traveling tune
Rolling over the bridges and viaducts
One could almost hear them say,
    "You're fucked   You're fucked"
As storm clouds gathered over Boca Chica Bridge.

A single piece of iridescent Conch shell
Lay on the roadway
Dropped by a brown pelican
When he flew over US Highway I.
Jagged and sharp, It ripped through Brenda's tires. Her
    car careened off the beaten path
Spilling its contents of secret tapes,
The yellow Speedo and a 12 inch dildo
Into the mangroves.

It was late, all rental car agencies
In Marathon were closed for the night
When the tow truck dropped Brenda
At Old Halls Fish Camp Resort.
The night clerk stood barely 4 feet tall.
Dressed in leather, chains and a rainbow scarf
Tied around *his* pimpled neck.
She greeted Brenda with a sly wink and
A sweaty hand shake that lingered too long.
She passed Brenda the room key.

"It's kinda chilly tonight Honey.
Let me know if you need anything."
Smiling, as visions of the roofie-laced sugar plums
He'd stashed in her room danced in *his* head.
    "MAY THE <u>FARCE</u> BE WITH YOU."

February 2007: Federal Courthouse, Key West, Fl (Wishful Thinking)

Nicaraguan Serenade
(Sing to the melody of "Old MacDonald Had A Farm")

Old MacMorgan had a farm
        E I E I O
Put all his money in that farm
Had to let his legal staff go.

And on this farm he had some cows
        E I E I O
Paid for by the $$$ he saved on payroll
        E I E I O
With a moo moo here and a moo moo there
Here a moo, there a moo, everywhere a moo moo
Old MacMorgan had a farm
In the Nicaraguan Hills

JeanMarie's check was worth three heifers
        E I E I O
And JulieAnne's salary paid for six goats
        E I E I O
With a bah bah here and a bah bah there
Here a bah, there a bah, everywhere a bah bah
Old MacMorgan had a farm
In the Nicaraguan Hills

Ms. MarilynSue's cache brought in twenty ducks
        E I E I O
With a quack quack here and a quack quack there
Here a quack, there a quack, everywhere a quack quack
Old MacMorgan had a farm
In the Nicaraguan Hills

Now he waits for more money to come in
And other financial factors
When he recoups DonnaLou's fees
He'll go out and buy himself a tractor.

Old MacMorgan had a farm
In the Nicaraguan Hills
E I E I O

(Florida is an "At Will" Employer's State; Fired after 16 years of loyal service with no notice)

3/26/08

Kli Kli

I heard the first call of the Kli Kli Hawk this morning.
The shrill sound of the bird
Cut through the quiet of sunrise
Jarring me out of the in-between world
    of sleep and waking.
        Kli Kli . . . Winter is coming.

With a smile, I greeted an old friend.
For a Conch, this is a comforting sound.
The first call of the Kli Kli is a welcomed
    announcement
That the heat of Summer is finally over
And promises that the cool of Winter is on its way.

The first call of the Kli Kli
Reminds us of nature's life-affirming cycles.
Every year without fail this tiny sparrow hawk journeys
From Alaska and Newfoundland to the Florida Keys
Demonstrating his own instinctive rhythm of life.

In these fearsome times of snipers and terrorists,
When the world is once again on the brink of war,
It is good to know that some things do not change.

The phone rings
Jarring me again into wakefulness.
It is Cousin Artie
With news that Uncle Arthur has just made
His final journey home.
        The last call of the Kli Kli.

Life and Death – Time and Seasons
    Kli Kli   Kli Kli

Conch Name: Kli Kli Hawk
Common Names: American Kestrel, Sparrow Hawk
Scientific Name: Falco Sparverius

A poem for Uncle Arthur Gregory, A Key West Shrimper

11/2/02

Clouds
(Eulogy for Mario Sanchez)

I knew a man, a very gentle man.
He carved boats that sailed
And fish that swam
    Inside the clouds.
He told me he liked to carve
The things that gave him joy
    Inside the clouds
So that his art would
Make people smile.

From young man to old
Standing under the mango tree
He created his primitive art
First on rumpled brown grocery bags
Then carving the figures
With homemade tools
On discarded scraps of wood.

My grandmother knew
This gentle folk artist.
She grew up listening to his father
Read aloud newspapers
And Shakespeare plays in Spanish
While she worked, starting at the age of nine
In Key West Cuban cigar factories

Later, when I was grown
I came to know this gentle man
And his kind family.
Visiting their home on a narrow street
    In Old Gato Village.
Just one house down Louisa street
From where he was born.

There was good food, good friends, good times
And always that mischievous twinkle
In his eyes (even at the end).

So long my friend, you rest now.
Not many people leave
Such a rich legacy of our island history
To be enjoyed for generations to come.

I will not grieve your passing
    (too much).
For I can still see your gentle smile
    Inside the coulds.

"My art is simple, but it pleases"
Mario Sanchez
October 7, 1907 – April 28, 2005

4/28/05

Sweet Lorraine

An old mahogany tree
Lives in the military cemetery
On White Street.
In October 2005, Hurricane Wilma visited
Ravaged the island,
Flooded our homes
And split that tree in half.
One half died – the other survived.

She stood there for several months,
The remaining branches, withered and bare.
Seemed like the storm had ripped her heart out.
There was a large gaping hole in the center
Looked like her innards were exposed
She was a sorry, sorry, sight

Then, in December and January
We were blessed with lots of rain.
Odd timing, we all thought.
This is supposed to be the dry season.
In time, the hole crusted over,
New leaves popped out
Looking like poodle puppy tails.

That was a year and half ago.
I walked by the old mahogany tree last night.
There she stood, branches held high,
With more respectable leaves now
And my heart felt glad.
What a survivor!
With so little of a heart left
She's gonna make it.

She's got deep roots here – Several generations
Good reasons to stay – A strong life-supporting foundation.

I thought about my Cousin Lorraine
Lying in a hospital bed in Miami
Far away from family and friends
Clinging to life with tubes and stents,
Breathing machines keeping her going.
So I named the tree Sweet Lorraine
Cause if this tree could survive
With only part of a heart
So would my cousin.

We could all learn a lesson
Of hope from that old tree.
Hang on to life – Keep on going.
As long as that spark of life is lit,
Miracles can happen.
God knows I love that tree
And my Sweet Lorraine.

4/22/07 (Earth Day)

Postscript 5/4/07
Lorraine Burchell Castillo passed over into the loving arms of our Father on May 2, 2007.
The Mahogany tree stands as her living memorial.

I Can See Cuba From My House
(Reflections after the vice-presidential debate 10/5/08)

Gosh Darn, Dog Gone It
You betcha, I'm gonna
Jump right on it.
The John McCain bandwagon
That is,
TV interviews and VP Debates.
Katie Couric you can kiss my ass
As I plow through those
Presidential Gates (in 2012).
And, I pledge
On my children's' scholarships
I'll never wear a pantsuit
(Unless the RNC pays for it)
Watch my lips
They're ruby red
And weather-girl – broadcaster smiling
If you believe anything
That comes out of this bitch's mouth
You should be thrown off
The Mallory Dock pilings.

Father Anthony

He was a man of many names.
Some not so kind, I'm sure.
You may have known him has Captain Tony.
I knew him as Father Anthony.
Most nights you could find him tending bar
In his downtown meeting hall
Just off the corner of Greene Street and Duval.
Where nightly lectures on love and life took place.
Father Anthony's sermons were always delivered
With a gleam in his eye and a smile on his face.
Many different kinds of games
He has played throughout the years.
I do believe that Father Anthony
Steps to the sound of distant drums.
His brethren gathered round him
Each night in loyal admiration
To drink the wine of his own
Special kind of communication.
From the tip of his graying head
To the bottom of his dirty bare feet,
He was a man of hidden courage.
He did not go down in defeat.
The sick, the hungry, the busted
Sought him out in their hour of need
They called him Captain Tony
I called him Father Anthony, yes indeed.
                                              Amen

1976 Capt Toni's Saloon
Published in Solares Hill

Child at Play

My makeup is in the toilet,
Spilt milk upon the floor,
Cookie crumbs on the mattress,
Chocolate finger prints on the door.

These telltale clues are evidence
There is a child at play.
Holding my breath, I pray
For patience to see me
Through this day.

When this day is over,
And he's bathed and tucked in bed.
All the funny infuriating things he's done
Go tumbling through my head.

As I stoop to kiss his cheek good night,
He gives me a sleepy smile.
This quiet moment of peace and joy
Makes it all worthwhile.

Tomorrow, armed with Band-aids and Kleenex
I'll ward off those child rearing blues.
But for tonight my little one sleep tight.
Remember, I love you.

Vincent Bruner Gregory
Age 2, 1971

Places and Events

The Monroe Theater
623 Duval Street, Key West, FL, built 1890s
It's Cool Inside

In the 1890s Vaudeville and Burlesque played here.
Giving the island people a taste of the outside world.
Conchs, dressed in their Sunday clothes
Paid 35 cents to see these risqué shows.
Now she sits in tatters and her marquee doesn't flash.
Just another worn out theater showing x-rated trash.
       But, it's cool inside.

During the early 1900s
When the silver screen first hit this town
My mother learned to play the piano here
Listening to Mrs. Piodela
Plunk out old silent movie backgrounds.

In the 1940s when I was just a kid,
It was here that I learned to dream,
Watching Walt Disney films.
On Saturdays there was Zorro,
The Lone Ranger and Tarzan.
The theater was warm then
With the sound of children's laughter.

In the 1950s when ponytails and bobby socks
Were all the rage.
I would sit in her darkened balcony,
Experimenting with teenage necking games.

One October night in the 70s at Guild Hall,
I viewed an artist's wares.

He had chosen as his subject
this old theater in disrepair.
The painting showed the same marquee
Of movies that ran for at least ten years,
Deep Throat and *The Devil in Miss Jones.*

$95.00, the price on the framed artwork read –
Cheap for such a place.
She once stood proud and regal.
She once had style and grace.
Now she sits in tatters and her marquee doesn't flash.
Just another worn out theater
Showing x-rated trash.
                                      But it's cool inside
                                      So very, very cold . . .

October 11, 1976
Guild Hall, Key West, FL

Published in Key West Arts Review

Key West Sunset

Framed by pink tinted clouds
Sunset seemed softer today.
Sitting on Mallory Dock
Letting my cares slip away.
In the quiet of the approaching evening.
The minutes flew by one by one.
Lost in a communion with the setting sun.

When I finally became aware of my surroundings
I do not know.
Eventually I saw the others around me
Enjoying the sunset show.
I felt the presence of these people –
The sights, the sounds, the smell of them.
Tourists with all their talk of business back home.
The smell of newly bought island perfumes.
The squeaks of tropical sandals being broke in.
The young people and the mellow strumming of guitars
With their own unique smells of incense and herbs.

All these things broke my reverie,
But, only for a brief moment.
Then, the sun peeked out from behind a dark cloud.
Streamers of light bounced off the water in the harbor.
There, rolling out to greet me
Was a golden carpet of sunshine
Rising and sinking with the oceans flow.
My spirit now set free
Floated up this illuminated pathway
And melted in the fire of the sun.

Mallory Dock 1976

House of Dreams

The house surrounded me
Like a soft shawl.
This house, like none other
I have seen.
Stands as a stately monument
To one man's hopes and dreams.
As I moved through high-ceilinged rooms,
My spirit traveled back in time.
When this house was just an embryo
In the architect's mind.
I watched as the ship's carpenter
Carved strong woods into stairwells
And window casings.
His hands gently smoothing rough lines
As if a lover he was embracing.
Painters and masons added their artistry
To build a home of grace and style.
Their masterpiece has survived
For a long, long while,
Through one generation to another.
Giving comfort to those
Who sought shelter here,
Like a devoted mother.
As I walked away from her, I cried,
Not from sadness, but from pride.
For I knew even after I had departed
That a part of me would remain inside.

Dedicated to all historic Conch houses
1975

October Smoke

Two-and-a-half tons
Two-and-a-half tons
They found it on a boat
Making one of those secret runs.
That nasty little weed, Maryjane
Was what it was.
My God, that is one hell of a buzz.
Now the men from the S.O.*
Were in quite dilemma.
What to do with stuff?
And, it had to be done in a huff.
If word leaked out down by Mallory Square,
Every freak in town would be there.
Standing by the side of the city dump,
Acting mighty strange.
Praying that the direction
Of the wind would change
So, they put the evidence
In a U-Haul It truck.
All the detectives and criminalists
Went along for good luck.
Up, up it went
In a big cloud of smoke.
The air was so heavy
Everyone began to choke.

After everything was said and done
I guess you could say
The boys from the S.O*
Had a little fun.
Because I could swear
As I watched them leave
The city dump.
Each and every one of them
Were smiling like chumps!

(*Monroe County Sheriff's Office)

1973 First Big Drug Bust in the Keys

Two Windows and a Door

Door to the middle or Door to the side
None of them were more than 20 ft wide.
High peaked roofs with shiny metal shingles,
Large open porches where folks could mingle.
Why did it take me so long
To learn my Cuban-American history?
I must have walked by those houses
Hundreds of times as a child
But their story remained a mystery.
Finally I learned about the 5 Varela boys
Who came from Cuba on a big sailing ship.
Made a living rolling cigars
That were shipped around the world.
Mr. Gato had a good thing going
Made lots of money and it sure was showing
In the many factories
And worker's houses surrounding.
They even named a village for him
As the neighborhood's founder.
Street cars, hospitals and
    Cigar Maker Cottages
This was the city of my uncles and grandfather.
5 of them lived in a 2 room flat
Till they each met and married Island Girls
And moved into their own
    Two Windows and a Door.
And me in my ignorance
Came back to Key West
To live in Grandpa's house
Not knowing how old it was
Or the tremendous impact

The Cigar Industry had on this island city.
Through the years those
    Cigar Maker Cottages
Went through a lot of renovations
Now it'll cost you a cool million to own one
With a pool and privacy fencing.
Sometimes at night when I walk
Through these cracked and aging streets,
A breeze comes up from Old North Beach.
I catch the sound of Domino chips
Banging on a kitchen table,
Or hear the rhythm of a conga drum
And, I know . . . I'm home . . .In my own
    Two Windows and a Door.

3/2/09

Battle Hymn of the Harbor Reef
(Why Conchs Don't Go Down Town)

White legs & Banlon socks
Tell me that
Another cruise ship just docked
Down by Mallory Square.

White legs & Banlon socks
Walking by Duval Street shops
Keep the merchants happy
Selling sleazy t-shirts
And made-in-China junk.

I smell the haze
Of stale beer and cheap liqour
That hangs over the street
Like a black mourning veil.
For us, she died a long time ago.
Trampled by so many "strangas"
Getting drunk on Duval Street.

Her bones lay
Dried and exposed
On the dirty, piss-stained sidewalks
Like the sagging rib boards
Of that old rotting ship
On Wisteria Island.

White legs & Banlon socks
Walking now a little quicker
Gotta get back to the boat in time
Don't want to miss that
Early call dinner.

Can you hear it
Above the din of mopeds and trolleys?
It's the melody of her funeral song:

"This is my island in the sun
Made for me by my father's hands
All my days I will sing and praise
Of her shining waters and shifting sands."
    Harry Belafonte (paraphrased)

8/25/11

Diamonds on the Water

High upon this lofty perch
Under the tree of life
I watch the sunlight
Gently skipping across the
Whitecaps below.
A swift glance from the bluff
See the sunbeams
Dance in the wind
Creating prisms and rainbows on
The blue ocean carpet.
How many lifetimes
Has this wondrous scene beguiled
Playfully teasing to mesmerize.
    Diamonds on the Water
The boat motor drones securely
Whipping up the water behind its propeller
Into frothy foam.
Delight in watching once again
As the liquid plume rises higher and higher
Finally capturing the sunlight
Then,
Raining down a fine gossamer mist
Of cool white glistening specks
That fall upon the sea
And melt into
    Diamonds on the Water
From the porch of a favorite
Beachside restaurant
A shimmering path of sunlight
Greets me with flecks of gold
Here and there

One upon one – to the thousands
Sculpting smooth, shining alabaster arms
Inviting me, tempting me onward
to the endless horizon.
    Diamonds on the Water

4/26/2010

Bolita Vacations

You could take a ferry
Park your car in the line.
Or, you could take an airplane
Got there in a jiffy, feeling fine.
They'd greet you at the airport
With rum punches and ruffled dancers.
Whatever way you got there
You always had a good time.

When I was just a little girl,
My mother said to me (on more than one occasion)
Come on Juana Maria
Pack your suitcase. I won Bolita*
'Tis Cuba we will see.

Mama's bookie was "Te Ta"
A slender man who walked with a limp
Always had an unlit Cuban cigar in his mouth.
I knew when he knocked on our door
We were headed south.
$100, $200, $500 bills were paid
A Cuban vacation was cheap in those days.

We stayed at the Hotel Nationale and
Mama drank daiquiris at Hemingway's favorite bar.
Watched voodoo rituals with chickens
And ponytailed exotic dancers
At the casino Tropicana.
Saw beautiful mountains, waterfalls and rivers
That winded through lush tropical valleys.
I was too young to understand

About the beggars in the streets
Or the perfumed ladies in the alleys.
Too distracted by the gold jewelry
That was sold in carts
On the marbled steps of the capitol.

Havana and Key West are connected
With strong family ties,
And a Cuban culture we share.
Now separated by a 50-year embargo
That's brought nothing but despair.
Sometimes when I'm asleep, I dream
That I'm eight years old.
Stowed away on a freighter hauling cargo
Drifting on the Gulf Stream.

When man's politics has run its course
And wiser hearts and minds prevail
You'll see me in Cuba again.
Cha   Cha   Cha. . .

August 8, 2010

*Bolita is an illegal Cuban lottery. In the 1950s the numbers were thrown in Havana and broadcast via radio to South Florida. The sounds of the winning numbers could be heard on most Key West streets. Bolita is still played in South Florida to this day.

Louisiana 2005
(8/29/05 Hurricane Katrina)

What has happened down here is the levees broke
Flooded out the homes of a lot of poor folk.
Hurricane rained all day and blowed all night
Too many people stayed in town
No way to get out.
20 feet of water in the streets of New Orleans

She tried to wash us away,
She tried to wash us away.

People walked to the Super Dome
With suitcases in their hands
No cars, No buses – that's all they had.
They waited one day, two days, five
No food, No water
Some never made it out alive.
20 feet of water in the streets of New Orleans

She can't wash us away,
She can't wash us away.

President George W. came down on a plane
A little sun-tanned, vacationed man
With a pack of lies in his hand
Hugging black children
To show the nation how much he cared.
But, he visited another state.
Must've been too scared
To face all them poor black folk
Doomed in the Super Dome.
20 feet of water in the streets of New Orleans.

She won't wash us away,
She won't wash us away.

FEMA made a lot of promises
That didn't come through
Now collecting dead bodies
Is all they can do.

**Louisiana, Louisiana
We're here to stay,
We're here to stay.**

Turtle Mystery Of 1948

Prologue:
"How much is that doggie in the window,
The one with the waggily tail.
How much is that doggie in the window.
I sure hope that doggie's for sale."
   (Popular song 1948)

At the foot of Solares Hill
Where it runs into Windsor Lane,
There was a bodega known as
Johnnie's Grocery in 1948.
Lots of thing went on that nobody
Talked about at Johnnie's.
Where, in a hidden back room
Heavy with the scent of Cuban cigar smoke,
Men played dominos and bolita.
The alcohol and bullshit flowed freely
Without license.
The wives didn't care
'Cause they always knew where
Their men were.

In September that year
A hurricane (unnamed in those times)
Blew across this little dot of land.
Blew so hard that the turtles
Broke out from the kraals
Down by Thompson's Dock.
All those turtles waiting for slaughter
Had a little free time
Swimming in the stormy waters.

The Miami paper wrote,
    "More than 200 giant turtles went to sea."
No one confessed to knowing
The secret truth of that turtle mystery.
You see, the Miami paper had it wrong.
Cause the hurricane blew north
Into the Gulf of Mexico coming in.
But, on the backside
After the kraals broke through,
It blew to the South going out
Causing the storm surge to flow down
To the cemetery collecting in a pool
At the foot of Solares Hill,
Forming a different kind of pen for
    The Turtles of 1948.

The water was knee deep
When the neighbors came out of their houses.
And, much to their gastronomical delight
Found huge, green turtles swimming in the street.
The smell of turtle stews and fried steaks
Filled the air .
As usual the Bubbas said nothing
Not to the reporter, not to the insurance man,
Not even to their priest.
On that hot and muggy star lit night
There was a quite a turtle feast
    On William Street.

Now, I'm not saying that
Eating turtles today is O.K.

But, as my old Conch friend "Blinkie" would say,
Rubbing his belly and sucking his teeth,
It's mighty fine eating when you are   hun g r y
With no refrigeration.

6-7-11

**Sources:*
The Miami Herald, Thursday, Sept. 23, 1948
Tom Hambright, Historian, Monroe County Library
Madeline Dowdell, my sister, seven years old in 1948

Philosophy

Reality & Dreams

When these karmic chains
That bind me to this ground
Have all been worked away
By lessons of laughter and tears.
Then, only then, will my restless spirit
Be set free – heaven bound.

Up through the clouds and sky of blue.
Past the ionosphere, moon and stars.
There in the fathomless void of space,
Somewhere between the galaxies,
I will wait for you.

Then, together again
Joining hearts and hands
We will fly throughout the universe.
We'll visit every star system
And watch as new worlds are born.
We'll leave no light unseen.
Our love will shine across eternity
As no sun has ever shone.
Guiding others through the fantasy of death
To the reality of their dreams.

1973

Dance On

Dancing lady
Whirl across the floor.
Music so pulsating and loud
You forget who you are.
The others in the room
Are not aware
That you are no longer there.
Now, dancing among the stars
Going back to times
When you danced provocatively for kings
In tents gently swayed by desert breezes.
Breathing in the ancient incense
You drown in a sea of intoxicating fragrances.

Getting lost is a new awakening.

The dance has ended
Once again, your feet touch the ground
In your soft brown eyes
A distant light still shines.

Dance On . . .

A regression at The Monster,
an old night club in Key West, FL
1974

Ride the Wind

On some magical evening
When your mind is quiet
With no place to go
   Ride the wind.

She is right outside your window
Gently stirring the pine trees.
If you listen carefully,
You will hear her persistent call.
Do not hesitate
   The wind waits for no one.

She will meet you where fleecy clouds
Pause only for a moment.
Surrender your spirit into her softness.
Whirling, tossing, turning
Cradling you in her arms, off you will go
Slowly at first, then racing, spinning, twirling
Through the sky.
"Where to," she asks? Anywhere . . .

To Morocco
Where hooded figures walk
Between the shadows of ancient buildings.
See the African moon rise above the sea.
Do not get caught in its silvery net of light.
   The wind is restless.

To the mountains
Peeking down from this majestic lookout
As storm clouds gather.
See lightening send fiery sparks

Down to the valley below.
Do not get spellbound
    The wind is uneasy.

To Venus
Where those who have departed our earth plane
Wait to greet us.
Visit with kindred spirits for awhile.
Do not get delayed
By too much conversation.
    The wind is impatient.

When the ride is ended
And you're neatly tucked in bed,
The wind will settle down for a well deserved rest
In that secret place where she hides
So the rain cannot find her.
Do not be sorry to see her leave
    The wind will return.

On some magical evening
When your mind is quiet
With no place to go.

1975

Midnight Butterfly

Moonlight on the bridge
Transformed the hard concrete and steel
Into a mystic thing of splendor.
The soft silvery net of light
Gently caressed the bridge
Making it come alive, breathing, pulsing.
The swift current below
Became a flowing silver carpet
With specks of liquid diamonds
Sparkling in the moonlight.
The tropical October wind
Tugged playfully with my hair,
And gave a chilled crispness
To the air.
My heart opened and took in the magic.
Right before my eyes
The bridge became a huge glistening butterfly.
He hovered for only a moment,
Wings extended, ready for flight.
Glancing back at me I heard him say,
"Come away with me Earth Child,
For I can free your soul
And take you to stars uncharted."
In my ignorance, I feared the unknown.
In just an instant,
The lovely creature departed.
Now, I am left behind
Standing in the sand, alone.
How heavy this clay prison has become.

Bahia Honda Bridge Oct 1973

Morning Star

Morning Star shimmering
In the new day's mist
What is the secret of your being?
Is it divine love that
Brightens up the sky,
And, lifts you ever suspended
In the heavens?
Or, is it the selfless need of nature
Just to be?
Alas, I tire of this conjecture.
It is enough for me
That you are beautiful
Because you are.

Let everyone who feels
That he is one with Thee,
Know that he is also one with all others.

1974

The Storm

Welling deep within me
A storm is taking place.
A storm of overwhelming
Beauty, peace and grace.

Like a flower pulsing
Ready to burst forth in bloom.
The storm is restlessly churning
On the brink it looms.

Like a tiny seedling
Newly planted in the ground
Awaiting the cool raindrops
To put its tender roots down.

LOVE IS THE STORM,
The bloom, the flower
The true essence of my being.
When it blooms, I shall die
To live forever within my brother.

1974

Safe Harbor

It is good to have a safe harbor
To bring your battered ship of life
For safe docking from time to time.
People have been searching
For this secure lagoon since time began.
Some people think it exists
In another person.
Resting all their hopes and dreams
In the life of another human being.
What a heavy, heavy burden to bear.
There is a place of quiet serenity
Peace and grace.
A place free from fear.
It lies hidden deep within.
Until you have the courage
To embrace it, make it your own.
You have only to look within to find it.
Once you do,
No storm, no strife on earth
Can pull your ship from her secure berth.

1975

Listen To The Night

Last evening, I sat in the garden
And listened to the night.
The message that I heard
Lingers with me still.

The moon cast a silvery soft light
Over the swamp
While fireflies fluttered
In the mangroves.
I closed my eyes,
Shut off my ears
And listened with my heart.
The message that I heard
Lingers with me still.

The trees, the grass, the stars
All joined in the chorus.
The message that I heard
Lingers with me still.

Shall I tell you, my friend
Of what I heard?
Here it is in simple words.

Your fate is only as hopeful
As your will.
To be strong, yet not hard.
To be gentle, yet not weak.
To be open, yet not naïve.
To be kind, yet not fool hardy.
To be wise, yet still thirsting to learn.

With all the noise and rushing
Around of a busy day.
It is good to listen to the night.

1973

If I Were A Tree

If I were a tree,
I would stretch my arms out
Reaching for the sun.
Taking in the golden energy
I would turn it into sweet, sweet air.
I would have a halo of crisp
Green leaves for hair
Where robins and blue jays could nest.
My trunk, sturdy and strong
Would stand tall for all to see.
Squirrels and insects would
Make their homes inside of me.
My roots would tie me to the ground,
But, my thoughts would be heaven-bound.
With this mixture of air and earth,
I would be a place of shade and warmth.

If I were a tree,
Man would eventually cut me down
To make senseless things of me
To clutter up his earth and seas.
Man, with all his greedy games
Would soon have his skies dark and grey.
Then struggling for breath,
He would look back at the spot
Where I once stood
And hang his head in shame

1974

Mother Earth Said, AHH

Hot and scorching Mr. Sun did burn
With no rain for 186 days and counting.
All the leaves were turning brown.
Not so pleasant around these parts
Mother Earth was frowning.

It was just too hot
For the delicate flowers this year
So they passed by spring
Without a welcoming blossom.
The drought caused torment
To every living thing.

The lizards, bless their little hearts,
Would wait for me to water the garden.
Then, they would scurry out to the puddles
To quench their thirst.
It was so damned dry,
Sometimes you'd think Mother Nature was cursed.

Finally the storm clouds gather in the Glades
Thunder rolled and the heavens opened up.
Last night as I watched the rain begin to fall
I could almost swear
I heard Mother Earth say AHH!

1974

Romance

Romancing the Tides

There is an inherent belief amongst the Conchs
That if you did something really, really good
In a former life, you would be blessed
The next time around to be born in Key West.

Growing up on The Rock
Taught lessons on how to survive
By what the ocean brought in on the tides.
Some would say that the world
Came to Key West on the high tide.
Island Girls learned early on
How to make the most
Of Romancing the Tides.

The 1950s & 60s were the halcyon days
Of hot good looking sailors and fly boys.
Fifteen men to every woman
Thanks to the U.S. military.
My cousins all married military men
Had babies and moved to the real world,
Not particularly in that order.

The 50s also brought the Shrimpers
Fishing for pink gold.
When the wind was wrong
The waterfront bars were full of 'em.
It was easy pickings for native girls.
The Shrimpers spent freely, got real drunk
And seldom bothered you past midnight.
Of course, you had to lay low, stay out of sight
Until the tide and wind were right.
Wait for their boats to sail out of sight.
Then move on to the next high tide.

In the 1970s developers and their lawyers
Helped the female population have a good time.
A girl could start out at happy hour,
Have dinner, go to the theater,
Dance till dawn and end up at breakfast
Never spending one thin dime.

The 1980s tide ushered in
Jimmy Buffet's Margaritaville and the TDC.*
In a few short advertising years
Key West became an international vacation city.
It was the place to be
Crowded with high rollers and carpet baggers.

Alas, a girl must settle down some time
And move away for a little while
Just to see the rest of the world.
When the hormones start going crazy
And the night sweats kick in.
A Conch Girl just has to come home again
Where the sea breezes keep you cool
And the tide is always high.

(*Tourist Development Council)

7-3-11

Ice Cream on a Hot Sidewalk

Remember how it felt when you were a kid
On a hot summer day?
Visions of luscious chocolate ice cream cones
Were the only thing that could chase
The heat away.
So you would save up all the empty pop bottles
You could find.
Sometimes, it would take a whole week.
Then, to the corner grocery store
You would sneak.
Five cents, ten cents – you would count along,
As the grocer stacked the bottles,
Just to make sure he didn't cheat.
Money in hand,
Running around the corner and up the street,
So excited you could hardly speak.
Into the drugstore or the ice cream parlor
On the next block.
You could almost taste it now,
At the soda girl piled the last scoop on top.
Outside again, the sugar cone
Sparkled in the sunlight,
As you took your first taste.
Swirling your tongue around the melting edges.
You didn't want to waste one precious drop.
Then, your appetite got the best of you.
So, you lunged into it with one big swooping lick,
Up from the bottom all the way to the top.
This is where you should have stopped.
Because before you could do anything about it,
Your ice cream fell to the sidewalk

With a dull, disappointing plop.
Stunned and with the sweetness still in mind,
Your spirit took a downward plunge.
As you watched the ice cream melt,
You fought off the tears,
Shrugged your shoulders
And headed for the school yard to play.
You weren't aware of it
But, you learned an important lesson that day.
The years have passed by, twenty and ten.
You're a grown woman now.
Yet, you find yourself in a different
But similar situation again.
As you walk away from him.
Shrugging your shoulders,
You remember the lesson learned so long ago.
Fighting back the tears you say to yourself.
Some men are like ice cream on a hot sidewalk.

1976

Poof

Lay beside me now;
Let's make love with our minds.
Just set our bodies on **Giving**
And, we'll begin the climb.

Come inside and stay awhile
We'll not be bothered by time.
There are no walls or clocks in here,
No chains that bind.

Like curious children exploring secret caverns
That jut out beneath the sea,
Let our **Imaginations**
Open locked doors to set our spirits free.

Watch thought forms rupture to the surface.
We can grasp hold of a few ribbony tails
To skim over the shallows of Life
In a boat rigged with gossamer sails.

Loving thoughts will keep us on course
As we journey through the dark forests of our minds.
Step aside for thoughts of **Inspiration**.
They move like lightning bolts.

If we are truly adventurous
And our hearts are pure,
We can take a trip
In **Fantasy's** space ship.

As our bodies embrace,
Thigh caressing thigh, we'll get high.
So high that Mother Earth
Will shrink in size right before our eyes.

Courage will guide us to our destination
Far removed from where we started
To that mysterious place where Midnight Butterflies
Visit stars uncharted.

Clay prisons forgotten
We explode in a climax
Of sparkling firework lights,
And vanish into the fathomless void . . . **POOF!**

1977

We Are One

When the wind
Brushes lightly against your face,
If your heart is pure,
You will feel my soft embrace.

When the sun it all
Her splendor shines,
If you close your ears
And listen with your heart,
You will hear my joyous laughter.

When the rain
Lays her sweet mantle down,
If you close your mouth,
You will taste my salty tears.

When lightening slices through
The storm clouds,
If you close your eyes,
You will see my loving passion.

And, if you can journey
To the ends of the universe
Without ever taking one step,
You will know
That I am the wind, the sun,
The rain and the lightening.

You are never alone

We are one.

1973

Until We Meet Again
(Love at First Sight)

I knew him
But he not me.
I saw him
But he could not see.
I loved him
But he did not respond.
What strange webs life weaves
To create such strong bonds
That last time and time without end.
Perhaps just coincidence some would say.
I think not.
To be so moved by a perfect stranger.
To know him so completely,
Without his even speaking a word.
To be aware of this feeling so intense,
Yet he not knowing
Does not even sense.
A secret it will remain.
Until, I am sure
At another time, another place
We will meet again.

Circa 1973

Capture

Smiling to myself, I wait.

Until my prey weakens

And comes my way.

Lurking like a cat

I keep a watchful eye

While he ignorantly sleeps.

Watching, waiting until

He becomes aware

Of the ever present danger

And captures me!

1973

Phoenix

A coward she must have been
To be so frightened.
Or, perhaps just a very gentle soul
Who stood in awe while in his presence.
Having opened Pandora's Box,
She trembled when its contents were revealed.
How can one being possess so much feeling?
The intensity of it takes the breath away
And stops the heart from beating.
The moth was only scorched by the flame.
And now wonders
Will she ever have the
Courage and strength to get lost
In the fire of his soul?
Then, on the other hand,
Like the legendary Phoenix
She will arise,
Reborn in youthful freshness
From her own ashes.

1973

Intruder

Into my private world, he came.
With his needs and after-shave,
Gently carving his mark
In these small rooms
And in my heart.

Now, the walls echo with his laughter.
My crying is heard even in the after.
Our hopes and dreams linger still
In the lofty rafters
Of my private world.

I let him in reluctantly at first.
Then, more willing,
Eager to quench his thirst.
We shared a special moment
Transcended in time and space
In this, my private world.

A new day dawns, now he is gone.
Yet he still remains
In bittersweet memories
Of joy and pain.

The task at hand is not new,
The wiping away of every trace of him
To make my private world
Mine   alone   again.

1973

Getting Over Him

I cried all day when I packed up his things
And took them to his mother.
Didn't leave anything that belonged to him
Standing in my cupboards.
I cried a lot last night,
This morning, just a little.
Yes, I'm getting over him.
I'll soon be as fit as a fiddle.
I'll file his face and name away
Somewhere in the back of my mind
Along with the fond memories
And all the good times.
Tomorrow I'll start smiling again
Maybe even sing.
Round and round time whirls on.
There's something quite familiar
About this whole damned thing.
It seems I've been here once or twice before
Going through the motions
Of tying up the last few strings
That bind my heart and emotions.
Tomorrow I'll look for love once more
Starting out with a fresh new refrain.
For today, I'm satisfied
Just to be getting over him.

1975

When Love Dies In The Tropics

Falling in love in Key West
Is the same as in other
    Romantic places.
Your heart will still skip a beat
When he comes into the room.
Intimate walks on the beach,
Holding hands at an outdoor café,
Gazing into each other's faces.

The difference is
When love dies in the Tropics,
The heart does not stay sad
For very long.
The sun shines so brightly
    Sprinkling diamonds
On the blue green waters,
A welcomed distraction.

Orange-pink sunsets caress
Soft and warm
Like comforting arms.
Silvery moonlight reflecting
    Off metal roofs
Gently transports a broken heart
To a more peaceful location.

A golden sunrise
Peeks out from the ocean
Framed by mauve-tinted clouds
    Heavy with rain
Whispers the promise of a new day
That surely
    LOVE
        Will come again.

7-31-2011

Drifting

Drifting along like a bubble
Bouncing on foam-tipped swells
Slowly moving forward
Stopping here and there to smell
      Life's roses.

Way off in the distance
Just over the horizon, it waits
Like a magnet, pulling
In a steady, but snail-like pace.

Is it the power of the Sun
Or a ferocious sea monster
With gaping jaws
      Ready to consume?

Greet a bearded sea gull;
Dance on the waves for awhile.
With one eye on that far-off horizon
And a sly Madonna smile
      She drifts along.

1976

MEN

There are some men
Made for loving,
And some made for using,
Some made for liking,
Some made for abusing.

If I could take
All the men in my life.
Line them up side by side.
Scan the group for lovely light.
I wonder what I'd find?

I've known a few men in my life.
I've loved a few men in my life.
And, for better words that
I cannot think of,
I'll end this poem right now.

P.S. Love 'em, Love 'em, Love 'em
    Dirty Rats

1975

Holidays

December Lights

Red, Yellow, White and Green
The twinkling lights of Christmas
Bestow their own special gifts
To our December scenes.

By dressing up the streets
And telephone poles
They create a fairy tale illusion
To a world so often
Unfriendly and cold.

Walking past the decorated windows
One can almost hear
Their holiday message
"Merry Christmas"
This home is full of goodwill and cheer.

Reflections of candle light
In our churches
Surround the Madonna and Child
With a soft fiery glow.
Proclaiming the miracle
That took place so long ago.

But, no lights shine quite as bright
Be they electric bulbs or candle light
As the happy faces of children
On Christmas morn.
For in their innocent faces
Shine the world's best hope
Of Christmases yet to come.

My Christmas wish for you
Is that the light of hope
Will shine bright and clear
To ensure for you
A very Happy New Year.

Christmas Magic

It is magic you know.
This holiday of ours.
Why, what else but magic
Could so subtly, yet powerfully affect
A people with that temporary insanity
    Christmas Shopping.
The thoughts of giving and sharing
Seem to fill the air
With their own special vibrations.
Making this time of year
More beautiful than any other.
How wonderful it would be
If we could save a little of this
    Christmas Magic
To be tucked away
In a very secret place
In the heart of Man.
And, there it would sit,
Ready to work its spell on us
Whenever we need a little extra shot
Of love, or kindness or understanding
    All year through.

The End

Bridges

Passed over your concrete arches
Bathed in sunlight and salt air.
Said good-bye to the whiskered sea gull
Perched upon a fishing pier.
Thought I sensed a hint of melancholy
Behind his curious stare.

Watched each island glide by the window
In a palm frond and hibiscus blur.
The mainland crept up on me
With its noisy traffic whir.
As the ocean faded from my sight,
Tears proclaimed a silent farewell.

Many miles inland, I saw those old bridges
In a different kind of light.
Had they always stood there tempting
With a silent urge for flight?
Was I drunk from too much sunshine,
Perhaps blinded by the glare?
Too occupied with loving her
To hear their persistent dare.

1979

About the Author

JeanMarie Gregory, who writes under the pen name of J.M. Varela in honor of her Cuban-American roots, was born in 1946 at the Monroe General Hospital on Stock Island. Purist Conch historians will tell you that a person is not a real Conch unless born on the island of Key West. So Jean validates her Conch heritage with the fact that she was conceived on lower Duval Street in an upstairs boarding house – the daughter of Blanche Varela, an island girl, and John Collins, a Tennessee hillbilly carpenter who came to Key West to help build the Truman Naval Station. Those who know her say she will probably die dancing with the Comparsa on Duval Street. Before that happens, she wanted to preserve her poetic ramblings for friends and family. This book is the result. Jean was educated at Key West High School, Florida Keys Community College, the Theosophical Society, Native American medicine wheel gatherings, metaphysical study groups and through the various dramas of life. She has enjoyed careers as a social worker, advertising manager and medical paralegal in Florida and Seattle, Washington. Some of her earlier poems were published in: *Key West Ghosts: An Anthology of Key West Poetry*, *KW Arts Revue* and *Solares Hill*. Jean is a founding member of the Key West Poetry Guild (KWPG) established in 1975 by a group of local poets who shared readings at Ms. Jessie Newton Porter's Heritage House. She has watched the poetry community of Key West come and go over the years and is pleased with its renewed popularity. Jean is a prolific writer who feels that she is just now getting started with so many other stories to tell. Can book #2 be far behind?